Microwave
Non-Veg

Delicious EASY-TO-MAKE Recipes

Microwave Non-Veg

Delicious EASY-TO-MAKE Recipes

Sarojini Menon

JAICO PUBLISHING HOUSE

Ahmedabad Bangalore Bhopal Bhubaneswar Chennai
Delhi Hyderabad Kolkata Lucknow Mumbai

Published by Jaico Publishing House
A-2 Jash Chambers, 7-A Sir Phirozshah Mehta Road
Fort, Mumbai - 400 001
jaicopub@jaicobooks.com
www.jaicobooks.com

© Sarojini Menon

MICROWAVE - NON-VEG
ISBN 81-7992-628-1

First Jaico Impression: 2006
Fourth Jaico Impression: 2010

ABOUT THE AUTHOR

Mrs. Sarojini Menon shares with her readers 67 mouth-watering recipes gleaned from her experiences over 33 years. Since 1982 she has been conducting cookery classes encompassing a wide variety of cuisines. She is particularly known for her easy to follow and delicious recipes.

In the early 90's microwave cooking attempted to revolutionise cooking in India. Many Indian women and men gradually began to find the Microwave an ideal appliance to assist them in their busy schedules. Making the transition from the gas stove to the Microwave was challenging and not enough guidance was available. Realising this Mrs. Menon started conducting cookery classes using Microwave ovens, simultaneously advertising for brand names like BPL.

In this book Mrs. Menon has explained various recipes that can be effectively prepared using the Microwave.

CONTENTS

TIPS FOR THE USE OF MICRO-WAVE OVEN

1. Vessels to use:

    (a) On convection mode, combination mode, grill mode, dual mode and also micro mode.
        Borosil, Pyrex, Corelle, Corning, Arcopol, or Ceramic.

    (b) On Micromode only
        Micro safe plastic i.e. Cello, Brite, Monalisa, Cutting edge, Prince or Ceramic

2. Do not use any metal containers or glass containers with metal designs or lines.

3. If you partly cover the vegetables while cooking with plastic/glass lids or cling film, the cooking will be done faster. (do not use aluminium foil) in case of cling film give a cut on the film (centre or any side).

4. Rice and dal should be soaked minimum half an hour before cooking.

5. Most of the dishes cooked in the microwave should be given standing time. Some food that do not seem completely cooked when removed from the microwave will get cooked during standing time.

6. If you overcook the vegetables, it gets a rubbery texture. Undercooked is better than overcooked.

7. To reheat leftover chappattis — Take a moist cotton cloth wrap 8-10 chappattis and keep it in the microwave. It takes $1^{1}/_{2}$ to 2 minutes. Topmost chappattis will get heated up fast. This can be followed for heating leftover snacks like potato wadas, idlis and samosas. While reheating the rice, sprinkle some water and cover partly.

8. Small uniformly shaped pieces of vegetables will cook faster than large ones.

9. Stirring food once or twice or more depending on the cooking time, during cooking, helps to cook more evenly.

10. If you open the door midway to stir, press "start" switch once again after closing the door to continue cooking.

11. To get rid off food odour from microwave, put a piece of lime in a cup of water and microwave for about 1 minute on Micro high.

12. To defrost frozen vegetables, pierce the bag or loosen the container slightly.

13. Deep frying cannot be done in a microwave.

14. Whenever the combo mode or convection mode is being used, the oven should be preheated upto a temperature indicated in the recipe (method) before using.

15. Time for cooking may slightly vary, due to voltage fluctuations, nature, type of vessel used and the quality of food etc.

16. The ingredients should be at room temperature, if not the cooking time will slightly vary.

17. 1 cup = 200 ml

Give yourself some time to understand your Microwave.

BASIC COOKING

Roasting papad:
If the microwave is small (25 to 28 litres) invert a paper plate, pile up 5-6 lijjat papad, then Micro high for 1 minute 30 seconds. If the microwave is large (more than 30 litres) invert a borosil or plastic dish, place a paper plate and pile up 5 lijjat papads, then Micro high for 1 minute 30 seconds. (time varies slightly depending upon the thickness of the papad).

Pop corn:
If imported ready-made bag is used, it will take $2^1/_2$-3 minutes. If loose corn is used, take a handful of corn, put in a glass vessel, with butter and masala, cover with cling film (give a slash on the cling film) Micro high for 3-4 minutes. If butter and masala is not used put the same amount of corn in a plain brown paper bag (folded). Keep on Micro high for 3-4 minutes.

Making tea or coffee:
One cup of tea or coffee will take approximately $2^1/_2$ to 3 minutes (of course depending on cup size). Do not fill upto the brim.

Boiling milk:
Take a deep container, fill the milk upto 50%. Half litre milk takes about 4 minutes.

Roasting groundnuts
$^1/_2$ cup groundnuts. Put in a paper plate and Micro high for 2 to 3 minutes. Give standing time after which the skin can be peeled off.

Masala groundnuts:
Apply little oil, salt, chilli powder and repeat the same procedure.

Blanching tomatoes:
2 tomatoes cut into half, and put in a shallow dish and keep on Micro high for 1 to 2 minutes.

Blanching Badams:
Boil half cup water (Micro high for 1 minute), add the nuts, and Micro high again for 30 seconds. The skin peels off easily.

To Cook potatoes:
Medium size 5-6 potatoes. Wash and prick/slash with fork and Micro high for 7 minutes. Give standing time, then chop it or mash it according to the recipe.

Full Boiled Egg:
The egg should be at room temperature. Take one egg, add enough water to immerse the egg and keep for $1^1/_2$ to 2 minutes at slightly less power (80% power).

Chicken:
For all chicken preparations, Broiler Chicken is to be used. Otherwise, Cooking time will increase.

Chicken stock:
1 kg chicken or $^1/_2$ kg bone pieces, 1 onion grated crushed, 1 tsp each of crushed garlic and ginger, 1 tsp salt and 5 cups water. Remove skin of chicken, put it or bone pieces in the cooker along with all ingredients, cook under pressure for 15 minutes strain and collect the liquid which is known as stock.

Birishta:

Onions fried to dark brown colour (2 onions sliced + 1 tbsp ghee takes approximately 7 to 8 minutes on Micro high)

Note: Whenever any material is kept directly on the rack for cooking. It is advisable to apply some oil on the rack.

SOUPS

Hot, tasty and filling, a small meal by itself. Supplemented with warm buttered breads, or rolls, flavoured with your favourite butters becomes a good wholesome meal. So go ahead and enjoy bowls of hot steaming spicy soups.

CREAM OF FISH AND VEGETABLE SOUP

Serves: 3 people
Preparation time: 9 minutes

INGREDIENTS

- *100 gm fish fillets (cut into small pieces)*
- *1 medium size potato, turnip and carrot*
- *1 onion*
- *$\frac{1}{2}$ litre chicken stock*
- *1 tbsp butter*
- *$\frac{1}{2}$ tsp salt*
- *$\frac{1}{2}$ tsp pepper powder*
- *50 gm cream*
- *parsley or coriander leaves chopped for garnishing*

METHOD

1 Grate potato, turnip, onion, carrot and mix. Put in a vessel along with fish.

2 Partly cover and Micro high for 4 minutes, stirring in-between.

3 Blend in a blender.

4 Transfer the blended mixture to a dish add chicken stock, salt, pepper, butter, mix well and Micro high for 5 minutes.

5 Serve hot garnished with cream, parsley/coriander leaves.

FRESH MUSHROOM AND CHICKEN SOUP

Serves: 4 people
Preparation time: 17 minutes

INGREDIENTS

- *100 gm boneless chicken shredded*
- *6 to 8 fresh mushrooms, each cut into 4 pieces*
- *4 spring onions along with the green parts chopped fine*
- *1 litre chicken stock*
- *1 tbsp soya sauce*
- *1 tsp salt*
- *$\frac{1}{8}$ tsp ajinomoto*
- *$\frac{1}{2}$ tsp white pepper powder*
- *4 tbsps (heaped) corn flour*
- *$\frac{1}{2}$ tsp sugar*

METHOD

1 Put the Shredded chicken in a vessel, cook on Micro-High 3 minutes covering partly stir in between.

2 Put the mushrooms, Micro high 2 minutes covering partly.

3 Add spring onions, Micro high 1 minute

4 Add stock, soya sauce, salt ajinomoto, pepper, Micro high 8 minutes or little more till it boils.

5 Add corn flour mixed with little water and Micro high 3 minutes stirring in between.

SWEET CORN CHICKEN SOUP

Serves: 4 people
Preparation time: 16 minutes

INGREDIENTS

- *4 cups chicken stock*
- *1 cup cream styled corn*
- *¼ kg boneless chicken shredded*
- *4 tbsps (heaped) corn flour*
- *1 tsp salt*
- *¼ tsp ajinomoto*
- *½ tsp white pepper powder*
- *1 egg*
- *½ tsp sugar*

METHOD

1 Put the shredded chicken in a vessel, partly cover and cook Micro high for 3 minutes.

2 Add chicken stock, Micro high 8 minutes.

3 Add corn, salt ajinomoto, sugar and pepper powder and Micro high for 2 minutes.

4 Add corn flour mixed with water, Micro high another 3 minutes or till boils stirring in between.

5 Beat the eggs slightly, open the oven door and add to the soup (do not remove the vessel from oven) stirring continuously.

6 Serve with chilli sauce.

HOT AND SOUR SOUP

Serves: 4 people
Preparation time: 18 minutes 30 seconds

INGREDIENTS

- *1 cup shredded mix meat (prawns, chicken and ham in equal amounts)*
- *4 cup chicken stock*
- *2 tbsps each of finely shredded bamboo shoots, cabbage, carrot, capsicum and sprouted beans*
- *2 to 3 chinese mushroom sliced*
- *2 tbsps soya sauce*
- *4 tbsps vinegar*
- *4 tbsps corn flour*
- *1 tsp each of chilli powder and black pepper*
- *$\frac{1}{2}$ tsp each of salt, sugar and ajinomoto*
- *1 tbsp oil*
- *1 egg*

METHOD

1 Bring the stock to a boil (Micro high 8 to 9 minutes)

2 Add the meat, Micro high for 4 minutes

3 Add vegetables, Micro high for 3 minutes.

4 Add soya sauce, vinegar, salt, sugar ajinomoto and pepper.

5 Mix corn flour with water and add to the soup. Micro high 3 minutes (bring to boil).

6 Gradually mix-in, lightly beaten egg stirring continuously.

7 In a small vessel, add 1 tbsp oil, Micro high for 30 seconds. Put chilli powder, stir and add to the soup.

serve hot

WONTON SOUP

Serves: 3 people
Preparation time: 13 minutes

INGREDIENTS

- *2 tbsps flour (maida)*
- *$\frac{1}{2}$ tsp oil*
- *1 tbsp beaten egg*
- *pinch of salt*

  (Mix flour, salt, oil, add egg, knead to a soft dough wrap the dough in a polythene and refrigerate for 1/2 an hour)

METHOD

1 Cut cabbage into square or triangle pieces, cut carrots and bamboo shoots into thin slices, slice mushrooms.

2 Roll wanton dough into a thin round shape cut this into approximately 3 inch square pieces.

3 Put very little of the filling in one corner of each piece, roll it up, bring the edges together and bind with egg.

4 Put the stock in a vessel, Micro high for 7 minutes.

5 Put the wantons, Micro high 4 minutes partly covering.

FOR FILLING

- *1 tbsp cooked and chopped chicken*
- *$^1/_2$ tbsp chopped bamboo shoots*
- *2 to 3 mushrooms finely chopped*
- *$^1/_8$ tsp each of salt, sugar, ajinomoto and pepper*
- *(mix all the ingredients)*

INGREDIENTS FOR SOUP

- *3 cups chicken stock*
- *1 small carrot*
- *1 tbsp bamboo shoots*
- *4 to 5 mushrooms*
- *2 tbsps cabbage*
- *$^1/_2$ tsp each of salt and sherry*
- *$^1/_4$ tsp ajinomoto*

6 Add the vegetables, Micro high 2 minutes.

7 Add salt, ajinomoto, sherry and serve hot.

THREADY CHICKEN SOUP

Serves: 5 people
Preparation time: 16 minutes

INGREDIENTS

- *¹/₂ kg chicken shredded*
- *5 cups chicken stock*
- *1 tbsp alphabetic macroni or chopped plain macroni*
- *2 beaten eggs*
- *1 tsp salt*
- *¹/₂ tsp pepper*
- *¹/₈ tsp ajinomoto*

METHOD

1 In a vessel Micro high chicken stock for 10 minutes, add shredded chicken and macroni and Micro high 5 minutes.

2 Add salt, ajinomoto, pepper and Micro high 1 minute.

3 Add the beaten eggs stirring continuously.

RICE
PREPARATION

The best part about rice dishes is that you can make them as a main dish. Mixed with meat or chicken and vegetables of your choice they become a complete dish. Everybody will just love it. They are light, elegant and perfect to serve at lunch and dinner parties.

CHICKEN BIRYANI

Serves: 8 people
Preparation time: 38 minutes 30 seconds

INGREDIENTS

- $\frac{1}{2}$ kg chicken pieces
- 4 tbsps cashewnuts
- 1 tbsp raisins
- 1 large onion – finely sliced
- 2 bay leaves (tej patta)
- 500 gm basmati rice
- $3\frac{1}{2}$ cups water
- 1 tsp salt
- 3 tbsps ghee

METHOD

1 Grind masala ingredients together and marinate chicken pieces for 30 minutes.

2 In a vessel, Micro high 1 tbsp ghee for a minute, put cashewnuts, and raisins Micro high 30 seconds, remove and keep aside for garnishing.

3 In the same ghee, put onion Micro high 6 minutes, stirring in between and keep aside for garnishing.

4 In the same vessel, add the remaining ghee, Micro high 1 minute, put bay leaf and spices, Micro high 1 minute.

5 Add chicken Micro high 10 minutes.

6 Wash and soak the rice for $\frac{1}{2}$ an hour and drain out.

FOR MASALA

- *1 tsp garam masala*
- *1 onion chopped*
- *3 cloves garlic – crushed*
- *2" piece ginger – crushed*
- *$1^1/_2$ cup fresh curd*
- *1 tsp salt*

SPICES

- *4 cloves*
- *8 to 10 pepper corns*
- *5 cardamoms*
- *2" piece cinnamon*
- *$^1/_2$ tsp turmeric powder*

7 In a vessel, put rice, add $3^1/_2$ cup water, 1 tsp salt, Micro high 14 minutes. Cool.

8 In a vessel put layers of rice and chicken alternatively, the top layer should be rice. Sprinkle little water on rice at the top layer, pour 1 tbsp melted ghee evenly and Micro low (keep approximately at $^1/_3$ of the maximum power reading shown in the oven) for 5 minutes.

9 Take out from the oven and garnish with fried onion and nuts.

CHICKEN PULAO

Serves: 6 people
Preparation time: 24 minutes 30 seconds

INGREDIENTS

- *1 cup shredded chicken*
- *$1^1/_2$ cup basmati rice*
- *3 cups chicken stock*
- *2 medium size onions sliced*
- *8 pepper corns*
- *4 cinnamon stick*
- *4 cloves*
- *2 tsps salt*
- *4 cardamoms*
- *3 tbsps ghee*
- *3 bay leaves*
- *2 tbsps cashewnuts*
- *1 tbsp raisins*

METHOD

1 Put ghee in a vessel, Micro high $1^1/_2$ minute add onion bay leaf, pepper corn, cardamom, cloves and Micro high 6 minutes.

2 Put shredded chicken, Micro high for 3 minutes stirring in between.

3 Add rice (washed and soaked for $^1/_2$ an hour and drained) cashewnuts, raisins, chicken stock, salt. Micro high for 14 minutes, stirring in between once.

4 Give standing time for about 10 to 15 minutes.

MIXED MEAT RICE

Serves: 4 people
Preparation time: 21 minutes 30 seconds

INGREDIENTS

- *5 tbsps each of boneless chicken, prawns and ham or 200 gm of any one of these*
- *1 cup basmati rice*
- *3 spring onions*
- *1 tbsp soya sauce*
- *1 tsp salt*
- *$\frac{1}{8}$ tsp ajinomotto*
- *4 tbsps oil*

METHOD

1 In a vessel, put rice (washed and soaked in water for half an hour and drained) and $1\frac{1}{2}$ cup water and Micro high for 10 minutes. Give standing time 15 minutes minimum.

2 Cut the meat and onion into strips.

3 In a vessel put oil, Micro high for $1\frac{1}{2}$ minutes, put meat. Micro high for 5 minutes stirring in between.

4 Add spring onion, Micro high for 1 minute add rice, soya sauce salt, ajinomoto. Sprinkle little water, Micro high for 4 minutes stirring in between.

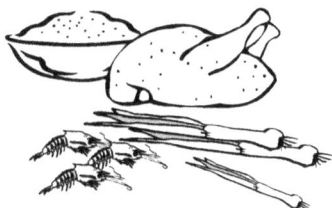

ARABIAN PULAO

Serves: 6 people
Preparation time: 40 minutes

INGREDIENTS

- *1 cup basmati rice*
- *250 gm mutton pieces*
- *2 eggs*
- *1 tsp coriandar seed*
- *$^1/_2$ tsp jeera*
- *1" piece ginger*
- *3 cloves garlic*
- *3 red chillies*
- *$^1/_4$ tsp nutmeg powder*
- *8 almonds*
- *1 tbsp raisins*
- *2 potatoes*

METHOD

1 In a vessel, put coriandar seeds, cummin seed, red chillis, Micro high 1 minute and grind along with ginger, garlic and mix this with curd to make masala.

2 Marinate the mutton in the above masala for 2 to 3 hours.

3 Hard boil the egg, (refer basic cooking) cut into half.

4 Cook potatoes, (refer basic cooking) cut into half.

5 In a vessel put 2 tbsp ghee Micro high 1 minute. Add sliced onion, Micro high 7 to 8 minutes stirring in between. Remove the onions (this is birishta) add blanched (refer basic cooking) and sliced almond, Micro high 1 minute add raisins, Micro high 30 seconds, remove and keep aside.

6 Make a fine powder of cinnamon cloves, cardamom and nutmeg.

- *2 onions birishta (fried to dark brown colour)*
- *2 green chillies sliced*
- *1 cup curd*
- *juice of half lemon*
- *$1/2$ tsp salt*
- *3 pepper corns*
- *1" piece cinnamon*
- *2 cloves*
- *2 cardamoms*
- *$1/2$ tsp saffron yellow colour*
- *2" piece raw papaya or tendron powder*

7 In a vessel, put 1 tbsp ghee, Micro high 1 minute, add marinated mutton and salt 2" piece of raw papaya Micro high 10 minutes stirring in between.

8 Add 2 tsp crushed fried onions, Micro high 2 minutes. Give standing time of about 15 minutes.

9 Wash and soak the rice for $1/2$ an hour and drain the water.

10 In a vessel put rice $1^1/_2$ cups water, $1/2$ tsp salt, Micro high 10 minutes give standing time 10 to 15 minutes.

11 Mix-in powdered garam masala to the rice along with lemon juice and saffron yellow colour.

12 Mix together onions, almonds and raisins divide into two equal parts.

13 In a greased vessel spread some rice then mutton on top, then potato and eggs and then one part of onion mixed with nuts. Spread the remaining rice balance of onion mixed with nuts sprinkle 2 tbsps ghee on top keep on Micro low. (approximately $1/_3$ of the maximum power) for 8 minutes.

FISH PULAO

Serves: 6 people
Preparation time: 23 minutes

INGREDIENTS

- 1$\frac{1}{2}$ cups basmati rice
- 1 pomfret – cut into pieces
- 2 onions
- 3 sticks cinnamon
- 3 cloves
- 2 bay leaves
- 1$\frac{1}{2}$ tsps salt
- 1$\frac{1}{2}$ tsps chilli powder
- 1 tsp cummin seed powder
- 2 tsps coriander powder
- 1 tsp garam masala powder
- pinch of turmeric powder
- 3 cups water
- 2 tbsps worcestershire sauce

METHOD

1 In a vessel put $\frac{1}{2}$ cup oil, Micro high 2 minutes, add onions and spices, Micro high 5 minutes.

2 Add the dry masala, salt and Micro high 1 minute.

3 Add pomfret, worcestershire sauce, Micro high 1 minute stirring in between.

4 Add the rice and water, cook on Micro high for 14 minutes stirring once midway. Give standing time of about 15 minutes.

PRAWN PULAO

Serves: 4 people
Preparation time: 29 minutes

INGREDIENTS

- *1 cup basmati rice*
- *1 cup prawns*
- *1 large onion chopped*
- *3 cloves*
- *3 cardamoms*
- *1" piece cinnamon*
- *$\frac{1}{2}$ lime*
- *$\frac{1}{2}$ tsp chilli powder*
- *$\frac{1}{2}$ tsp turmeric powder*
- *1 tsp coriander powder*
- *$\frac{1}{2}$ tsp salt*

GRIND TO A PASTE

- *1 onion*
- *3 flakes garlic*
- *1" piece ginger*

METHOD

1 Soak the rice for $\frac{1}{2}$ an hour and drain out the water. Cook in a vessel on Micro high for 10 minutes with $1\frac{1}{2}$ cups of water. Give standing time of about 15 minutes.

2 In a vessel put 2 tbsps oil, Micro high 1 minute.

3 Add the garam masala and chopped onion, Micro high 4 minutes stirring in between.

4 Add onion/ginger/garlic paste, Micro high 6 minute stirring in between.

5 Add chilli turmeric and coriandar powder and mix well.

6 Add prawns and salt cook on Micro high for 4 minutes.

7 Add rice, lime juice sprinkle little water mix lightly cook an Micro low (half of the maximum power reading shown in the oven) for 4 minutes.

MUTTON PREPARATION

These are very elegant and very tasteful recipes from juicy and tender mutton. They are given justice by the magic of thin gravy or with the hint of mint and coriander. You can make these recipes when you want to cook a very special dish for your family or when you want to impress your guests.

MUTTON AND SPAGHETTI CASSEROLE

Serves: 4 people
Preparation time: Combo-35 minutes, Dual-34 minutes, Micro-31 minutes

INGREDIENTS

- *250 gm mutton mince*
- *1 egg*
- *30 gm bread crumbs*
- *2 tbsps oil*
- *200 gm spaghetti*
- *750 gm tomatoes*
- *1½ tbsps maida*
- *1 tbsp butter*
- *1 onion*

METHOD

1 Wash the mutton mince, squeeze out water.

2 Add ¼ tsp salt and pepper each, mix in the egg, shape into small balls and roll in bread crumbs.

3 Place in a shallow dish, sprinkle 1 tbsp oil.

4 Micro high for 4 to 5 minutes and keep aside.

5 Take 1 litre water in a vessel and Micro high for 9 minutes.

6 When the water starts boiling add 1 tsp oil and salt each and the spaghetti.

7 Micro high for about 4 minutes, stir in between.

8 Remove, give 2 minutes standing time strain and keep aside.

9 Make tomato puree (cut

- *1 carrot*
- *$1^{1}/_{4}$ tsps salt*
- *$1^{1}/_{4}$ tsps pepper*

the tomatoes into small pieces, put in a dish along with 2 cloves of garlic and one chopped onion. Micro high for 4 minutes, cool blend in a liquidiser and strain)

10 Chop the onion and carrot.

11 In a dish, put butter, Micro high 30 seconds add chopped onion and carrot, Micro high for 2 minutes.

12 Add maida, mix well.

13 Add tomato puree, salt and pepper and Micro high for 5 minutes.

14 In a casserole dish, place spaghetti and mutton balls, cover with tomato puree.

15 Preheat the oven at 180°c and cook on combo mode at 180°c for 7 minutes or on Dual mode 150 for 6 minutes or on Micro high 3 minutes.

BROWN STEW
(WESTERN STYLE)

Serves: 6 people
Preparation time: 23 minutes

INGREDIENTS

- *500 gm mutton (cut into small equal size pieces)*
- *2 onions*
- *2 carrots*
- *2 potatoes*
- *³/₄ litre stock (mutton or chicken)*
- *2 tbsps maida*
- *1¹/₂ tsps salt*
- *1 tsp pepper*
- *3 tbsps oil*
- *2" piece raw papaya or ¹/₂ tsp tendron powder*

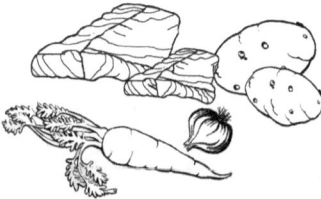

METHOD

1 Cut vegetables into small equal size pieces

2 Chop onions

3 In a dish, put oil, Micro high one minute add onion, Micro high 2 minutes.

4 Add stock, salt, pepper, mutton and 2 inch piece of papaya (tenderiser) or tendron powder.

5 Micro high 12 minutes partly covering

6 Add vegetables, cook on Micro high 5 minutes partly covering.

7 Add maida blended with little water and cook on Micro high 3 minutes, stirring in between.

8 Give standing time of 10 to 15 minutes.

SHEEK KABAB

Serves: 8 people
Preparation time: Combo-7 minutes, Dual-7 minutes, Micro-4 minutes

INGREDIENTS

- *1/2 kg minced mutton (squeeze out the water)*
- *1 tsp salt*
- *pinch of tendron powder*
- *1 tsp chilli powder*
- *1/2 tsp garam masala*
- *1/4 tsp nutmeg powder*
- *1 tsp dry methi (fenu greek) leaves*
- *2 tsps powdered poppy seeds*
- *2 tsps powdered cashewnut*
- *1 tsp crushed ginger*
- *1/2 tsp crushed garlic*
- *1/4 tsp orange red food colour*
- *1 tbsp each of chopped coriander leaves and green chillies*
- *1 egg*

METHOD

1 Mix all the ingredients except egg and grind to a paste

2 Mix in the egg refrigerate for half an hour to harden the mixture.

3 Divide the mixture into 16 to 18 portions

4 Apply little oil on the palm and make the shape of sheek kabab.

5 Preheat the oven at 180°c keep the kababs on the rack and cook on Combo mode at 180°c for 7 minutes or on Dual mode 150 for 7 minutes keeping the kababs on higher rack and turning after 4 minutes or Micro high 4 minutes.

(Note: Brush the kababs with oil after half of the cooking time is elapsed)

MASALA MEAT LOAF

Serves: 4 people
Preparation time: Convec-16 minutes 30 seconds, Grill-16 minutes
30 seconds, Micro-11 minutes 30 seconds

INGREDIENTS

- *¹/₄ kg mutton finely minced*

FOR MASALA 1

- *1 onion – chopped*
- *1 tbsp chana dal*
- *3 green chillies*
- *1 small bunch coriander leaves*
- *¹/₂ inch ginger sliced*
- *¹/₂ tsp chilli powder*
- *¹/₂ tsp turmeric powder*
- *³/₄ tsp salt*
- *few mint leaves*

METHOD

1 Soak the chana dal for 1 hour.

2 Place the meat in a vessel after washing and removing the water, along with chana dal, and all the ingredients for masala 1 except tomato ketchup, bread and egg.

3 Micro high 7 to 8 minutes, stirring in between (the meat should become dry) remove and cool.

4 Roast (Micro high 1¹/₂ minutes) the ingredients for masala 2 and grind finely.

5 Grind the cooled meat, powdered ingredients for masala 2, soaked and squeezed bread.

6 Mix in tomato ketchup and beaten egg.

- *1 tbsp tomato ketchup*
- *2 slices bread*
- *$\frac{1}{2}$ egg – beaten*

FOR MASALA 2

- *1 small piece dry coconut (copra)*
- *1 tsp poppy seed*
- *1 tsp charoli*
- *$\frac{1}{2}$ tsp black pepper*
- *1 small piece cinnamon*
- *2 cloves*
- *2 cardamoms*

7 Grease a loaf tin and tightly pack in the mixture pour 1 tbsp oil on the top surface.

8 Preheat the oven at 230°c and cook on convection. Mode for 8 minutes or Grill 8 minutes or Micro high 3 minutes.

(Caution: if Micro mode is being used, do not use Loaf Tin – use Microproof vessel only). Give standing time about 15 minutes.

MANPASAND KABAB

Serves: 4 people
Preparation time: Combo-7 minutes, Dual-7 minutes, Micro-2minutes
30 seconds

INGREDIENTS

- $1/_4$ kg mutton minced
- $1/_4$ tsp each of crushed garlic and ginger
- 1 small onion – chopped
- 3 to 4 green chillies chopped
- 2 to 3 tbsps flour
- $1/_4$ tsp garam masala
- $1/_2$ tsp salt
- $1/_2$ tsp pepper powder
- 2 slices bread

METHOD

1 Wash the mutton and drain the water. Mix all the other ingredients with mutton grind well and make small kababs.

2 Preheat the oven at 180°c keep the kabab on the rack and cook on Combo mode at 180°c for 7 minutes or on Dual mode 150 (keeping on higher rack) for 7 minutes turning after 4 minutes or on Micro high $2^1/_2$ minutes.

(Note: Brush the kababs with oil half way through the cooking time)

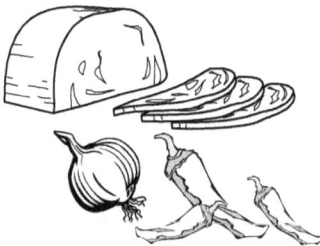

MEAT IN BOLOGNESE SAUCE

Serves: 4 people
Preparation time: 12 minutes

INGREDIENTS

- *250 gm minced meat*
- *1 onion chopped*
- *$^1/_4$ tsp crushed garlic*
- *1 carrot finely chopped*
- *2 slices bacon chopped*
- *1 tbsp chopped celery*
- *$^1/_4$ tsp chilli powder*
- *1 cup tomato puree*
- *1 tsp oregano or ajwain*
- *150 ml red wine*
- *$^1/_2$ tsp salt*
- *$^1/_2$ tsp pepper powder*
- *1 bay leaf*
- *2 tbsps oil*
- *1 tbsp butter*

METHOD

1 Put the oil and butter in a vessel, Micro high for 1 minute, add onion and garlic and Micro high 3 minutes.

2 Add Bacon, carrot celery. Stir.

3 Partly cover and cook on Micro high for 2 minutes.

4 Stir-in the meat chilli powder bay leaf, Micro high for 3 minutes, stirring every minute.

5 Add tomato puree, salt, pepper, oragano or ajwain, wine stir well, Micro high for 3 to 4 minutes partly covered. Stir in between.

SHAMMI KABAB

Serves: 4 people
Preparation time: Convec-9 minutes, Grill-9 minutes, Micro-5 minutes

INGREDIENTS

- $1/4$ kg minced meat – washed and drained
- 1 tbsp chana dal (gram dal)
- 1 small onion chopped
- $3/4$ tsp salt
- $1/4$ tsp red chilli powder
- $1/4$ tsp garam masala
- $1/8$ tsp haldi powder (turmeric powder)

METHOD

1 Put all the ingredients in a vessel and Micro high 3 minutes stirring in between. The meat should become dry.

2 Add $1/2$ tbsp each of chopped green chilli coriander leaves and ginger mix-in $1/8$ tsp garam masala.

3 Grind the kheema mixture to a paste mix-in half beaten egg and $1/2$ tbsp lime juice.

4 Make the filling with $1/2$ tbsp kaju chopped, $1/2$ tbsp kismis chopped little salt, red chilli powder, garam masala and 2 green chillies chopped.

5 Divide kheema mixture into 8 portions make flat round balls.

- $^1/_2$ *tsp crushed garlic*
- $^1/_2$ *tbsp cashewnuts (Kaju)*
- $^1/_2$ *tbsp raisins (Kismis)*
- *2 green chillies*

6 Preheat the oven at 180ºc keep the kababs on the rack, apply little oil and Convec at 180⁰c for 6 minutes or grill 6 minutes turning after 3 minutes and applying oil or Micro high 2 minutes.

MUTTON PALAK

Serves: 6 people
Preparation time: 33 minutes

INGREDIENTS

- *¹/₂ kg mutton pieces*
- *3 bunches spinach*

TOMATO MASALA

- *3 onions grated*
- *1 tsp each of crushed garlic and ginger*
- *3 tomatoes blanched and chopped*
- *4 tbsps oil*
- *1¹/₂ tsp each of salt and chilli powder*
- *¹/₈ tsp haldi powder*

METHOD

1 Wash spinach well, squeeze off excess, water, chop and put in a vessel Micro high for 3 minutes. Cool and grind.

METHOD FOR TOMATO MASALA

1 In a vessel put oil Micro high one minute put garlic and ginger, Micro high 1 minute.

2 Add grated onion Micro high 8 minutes stirring in between.

3 Add chilli powder garam masala and Haldi powder

4 Mix-in tomato stir well Micro high 3 minutes stirring in between

5 Add mutton, 1¹/₂ tsp salt 1 cup water, two pieces of 2" size raw papaya Micro high 15 minutes covering partly, stir in between.

- *1 tsp garam masala*
- *1 tbsp lime juice*
- *50 gm cream*
- *2" piece raw papaya or $^1/_2$ tsp tendron powder*

6 Add ground spinach, mix well Micro high 2 minutes, stirring in between.

7 Take out, add lime juice and cream, give standing time of about 15 minutes.

KHEEMA MUTTER

Serves: 6 people
Preparation time: 19 minutes

INGREDIENTS

- $^1/_2$ kg kheema
- 3 onions grated
- 1 tsp each of crushed garlic and ginger
- 3 good size tomatoes blanched and chopped
- 2 tbsps ghee
- $1^1/_2$ tsps each of salt and chilli powder
- $^1/_4$ tsp haldi powder
- 1 tsp garam masala
- 1 cup of peas (mutter)
- $^1/_2$ cup water
- coriandar leaves to garnish

METHOD

1 In a vessel put ghee, Micro high 1 minute add garlic and ginger, Micro high 1 minute.

2 Add onion, Micro high 8 minutes, stirring in between.

3 Add tomato, chilli powder, Haldi powder salt, garam masala, Micro high 3 minutes.

4 Add kheema, mutter and water, Micro high 6 to 7 minutes. Stirring in between.

5 Garnish with coriandar leaves.

ACHAR GOSHT

Serves: 4 people
Preparation time: 19 minutes 30 seconds

INGREDIENTS

- *250 gm boneless mutton*
- *3 tbsps oil*
- *1 cup fresh curd*
- *1 achar chillies (big size chillies)*
- *1 onion – chopped*
- *$\frac{1}{2}$ tsp jeera*
- *$\frac{1}{2}$ mustard seed*
- *$\frac{1}{2}$ tsp fenugreek (methi) seed*
- *$\frac{1}{2}$ tsp kalonji (onion seed)*
- *1 tsp coriander powder*
- *$\frac{1}{2}$ tsp each of garlic and ginger paste*
- *$\frac{3}{4}$ tsp salt*
- *1" Piece raw papaya or $\frac{1}{4}$ tendron powder*

METHOD

1 Marinate the mutton with curd, salt, chopped, onion, oil, coriander powder, ginger, garlic paste for 4 hours.

2 Slit green chillies lengthwise

3 Roast (Micro high $1\frac{1}{2}$ minute) and powder coarsely the jeera, mustard, fenugreek seed and kalonji. Add $\frac{1}{4}$ tsp salt, mix and fill in the chillies keeping aside a small portion.

4 In a vessel put the marinated mutton Micro high 15 minutes, along with 1" piece of raw papaya. Stir in between.

5 Add green chillies, balance of ground masala, a pinch of tandoori. Red colour, Micro high 3 minutes. Stir in between give standing time of 10 to 15 minutes.

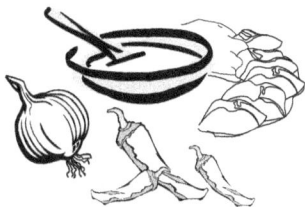

MUTTON SHAKUTI
(GOMANTAK STYLE)

Serves: 6 people
Preparation time: 35 minutes

INGREDIENTS

- $^1/_2$ kg mutton
- $^1/_2$ tsp cummin seed
- 1 coconut
- 1 tbsp coriander powder
- $^1/_2$ tsp pepper powder
- 2 to 3 pieces dhagad phool (stone flower)
- $^1/_4$ nutmeg
- 3 cloves
- 1" piece cinnamon
- 3 cardamoms
- 1 tsp khuskhus

METHOD

1 Cut the mutton to small equal size pieces.

2 Extract milk from half the coconut and keep aside. Grate the other half of coconut.

3 In a vessel, put grated coconut, cummin seed and coriander powder, Micro high 3 minutes stirring in between.

4 In a vessel, put 1 tbsp oil, Micro high 1 minute, put 1 onion sliced, Micro high 4 minutes, mix with the fried masala. (step 3)

5 Grind the rest of the spices with the fried masala. (step 4)

6 In a vessel, put 1 tbsp oil, Micro high one minute. Put the remaining sliced onion, Micro high 4 minutes stirring in between.

- $^1/_2$" piece ginger
- little tamarind
- 5 red chillies
- 1" piece turmeric
- 4 cloves garlic
- 2 onions – sliced
- $1^1/_4$ tsp salt
- 2" piece raw papaya or $^1/_2$ tsp tendron powder

7 Add the mutton, Micro high 4 minutes stirring in between.

8 Add the ground masala with $^1/_2$ cup water and 2" piece of raw papaya, salt, Micro high for 15 minutes covering partly. Stir in between.

9 Add coconut milk and tamarind pulp (put the tamarind in little water, soak for $^1/_2$ an hour and sqneeze our the pulp) Micro high 3 minutes, stirring in between. Give standing time 10 to 15 minutes.

CHICKEN
PREPARATION

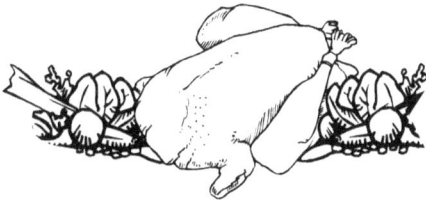

These tasty chicken preparation cooked with rich gravy that has succulent, juicy boneless pieces with a tangy taste or dry chicken preparation is fiery and sharp in taste. Served with rice or roti they are suitable for all occasion.

TANDOORI CHICKEN

Serves: 8 people
Preparation time: Combo-19 minutes, Dual-18 minutes, Micro-10 minutes

INGREDIENTS

- *750 gms chicken legs*
- *1 tsp each of crushed garlic and ginger*
- *6 tsps thick curd*
- *1 tsp garam masala powder*
- *1 tsp jeera powder*
- *2 tsps coriander powder*
- *$\frac{1}{2}$ tsp red chilli powder*
- *1 tsp salt*
- *$\frac{1}{2}$ tbsp chopped green chillies*
- *1 tbsp each of chopped mint leaves and coriandar leaves*
- *$\frac{1}{4}$ tsp orange red colour*

METHOD

1 Make gashes on the chicken legs and marinate with all the other ingredients mixed well for 5 to 6 hours.

2 Preheat the oven at 230⁰c and cook the marinated chicken legs on Combo mode at 230⁰c for 19 minutes or on Dual mode 450 for 18 minutes turning after 9 minutes or Micro high 10 minutes.

BUTTER CHICKEN

Serves: 8 people
Preparation time:
12 minutes 30 seconds

INGREDIENTS

- *1 kg chicken*
- *$^1/_2$ kg. riped tomatoes*
- *2 tbsps tomato ketchup*
- *4 tbsps powdered cashewnuts*
- *$^1/_4$ tsp each of salt and chilli powder*
- *1 tsp sugar*
- *1 bay leaf*
- *50 gm butter*
- *$^1/_2$ cup water*
- *100 gm cream*
- *1 tsp chopped green chillies*
- *few coriandar leaves chopped*

METHOD

1 Cut the chicken into small curry size pieces and follow the method for tandoori chicken

2 Chop the tomatoes and cook on Micro high with water and bay leaf for 4 minutes. Grind and sieve.

3 In a vessel Micro high butter for $1^1/_2$ minutes.

4 Fry cashewnut powder on Micro high for 2 minutes stirring in between.

5 Add the sieved tomato mixture tomato ketchup, salt, sugar and chilli powder, and Micro high 3 to 4 minutes (bring to boil stirring in between.)

6 Add the tandoori chicken pieces, Micro high for another 2 minutes.

7 Remove and add cream.

8 Garnish with chopped green chillies and coriandar leaves.

CHICKEN IN TOMATO GRAVY

Serves: 6 people
Preparation time: 18 minutes

INGREDIENTS

- *¹/₂ kg boneless chicken (cut into 1" pieces)*
- *¹/₂ tsp black pepper crushed*
- *1 tsp each of crushed garlic and ginger*
- *1 tsp red chilli powder*
- *few coriander leaves chopped*
- *¹/₄ tsp turmeric powder*
- *few curry leaves*
- *3 onions grated or crushed*
- *1 cup tomato puree*
- *2 tbsps tomato ketchup*
- *1 tsp coriandar powder*
- *1 tsp garam masala*
- *1 tsp salt*
- *4 tbsps oil*

METHOD

1 Marinate the chicken with chilli powder turmeric powder half of ginger garlic paste salt and keep aside 30 minutes.

2 In a dish put oil, add onions the remaining ginger garlic paste, coriandar powder, curry leaves, garam masala and cook on Micro high 6 to 8 minutes, stirring in between.

3 Add tomato puree and ketchup, cook on Micro high 2 minutes.

4 Add the chicken, coriandar leaves and crushed pepper corn.

5 Mix well and Micro high for 10 minutes.

CHILLY CHICKEN

Serves: 6 people
Preparation time: Micro + Convec-28 minutes, Dual-22 minutes,
Micro-20 minutes

INGREDIENTS

- *$1/_2$ kg boneless chicken –
  cut into 1 inch pieces*
- *3 tbsps soya sauce*
- *2 tbsps vinegar*
- *1 tsp sherry*
- *1 tsp chilli powder*
- *$1/_8$ tsp each of salt, sugar,
  ajinomoto*
- *garlic and ginger crushed*
- *1 big capsicum cut into
  strips*
- *5 green chillies*
- *$2^1/_2$ tbsps corn flour*

METHOD

1 In a bowl, mix all ingredients except capsicum and marinate the chicken for 3 to 4 hours.

2 Preheat the oven at 230ºC

3 In a glass dish, put 1 tbsp oil, keep the marinated chicken pieces and cook on Micro high 6 minutes and Convec 12 minutes or on Dual mode 450 for 12 minutes or on Micro high 10 minutes.

4 In a dish, put 2 tbsps oil, add 4 to 5 green chillies sliced, cook on Micro high for one minute, add 2 cups chicken stock, 2 tbsp soya sauce and Micro high till it boils (about 4 minutes)

5 Add the chicken pieces, capsicum, $2^1/_2$ tbsps corn flour dissolved in water, Micro high for 5 minutes stirring in between.

MUSSALAM MURG

Serves: 8 people
Preparation time:
Combo-19 minutes,
Dual-18 minutes, Micro-10 minutes

INGREDIENTS

- *1 kg chicken*
- *25 gm each of cashewnuts, raisins and coconut (dry copra)*
- *1 tbsp each of salt, chilli powder and garam masala*
- *$1/_2$ tbsp each of crushed garlic and ginger*
- *$1/_2$ cup thick curd*
- *juice of one lime*
- *few drops of saffron essence and saffron yellow colour*

METHOD

1 On the full chicken without skin, make deep cuts.

2 To the curd, add garlic, ginger and lime juice.

3 Leave to marinate for 6 to 8 hours.

4 Drain off the liquid

5 Mix garam masala chilli powder and salt. Apply this mixture on both sides of the chicken.

6 Grind cashewnuts, raisins and coconut to a paste using little water. Mix saffron colour and essence. Apply $1/_3$ of this mixture on the inner side of the chicken and the remaining $2/_3$ on the outerside.

7 Keep chicken on the rack or in a dish put dots of ghee on top.

8 Preheat the oven at 230°c and keep on Combo mode at 230°C for 19 minutes or Dual mode 450 for 18 minutes or on Micro high 10 minutes keeping in the dish – not on the rack.

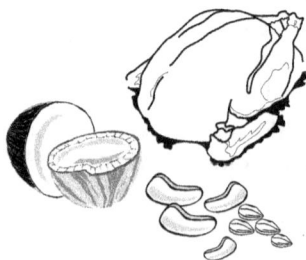

CHICKEN CROQUETTS

Serves: 4 people
Preparation time: Convec-21 minutes, Grill-21 minutes, Micro-17 minutes

INGREDIENTS

- *375 gm boneless chicken-shredded*
- *2 tbsps butter*
- *2 tbsps maida*
- *1 cup milk*
- *$1/_2$ tsp pepper*
- *$1/_2$ tsp salt*
- *1 onion chopped*
- *bread crumbs*
- *5 green chillies – chopped*
- *$1/_4$ tsp each of rushed garlic and ginger*

METHOD

1 Put the chicken in a vessel and Micro high for 3 minutes. Stir in between.

2 In another vessel, Micro high butter for 1 minute put garlic, ginger and onion and Micro high for 4 minutes add maida, mix well, put milk, Micro high 3 minutes stirring in between.

3 Add the chicken salt, pepper, green chillies, Micro high 4 to 5 minutes or till thickens, stirring in between. Remove cool make oblong shapes.

4 Preheat the oven at 180°C and keep on the rack, Convec at 180°C for 6 minutes or on grill 6 minutes turning after 3 minutes or Micro high 2 minutes.

HONEYED DRUMSTICKS

Serves: 8 people
Preparation time: 10 minutes 30 seconds

INGREDIENTS

- *4 chicken legs (about 750 gm)*
- *4 tbsps honey*
- *3 tbsps soya sauce*
- *1 tsp each of garlic and ginger paste*
- *$\frac{1}{2}$ tsp pepper powder*
- *$\frac{1}{2}$ tsp salt*
- *1 tbsp corn flour*
- *$\frac{1}{2}$ tbsp corn flour*
- *$\frac{1}{4}$ cup water*

METHOD

1 Mix together the honey, soya sauce, ginger, garlic pepper and salt in a bowl.

2 Wash and dry the chicken legs and marinate in the above mixture (step 1) 4 to 5 hours.

3 Keep the chicken in a vessel and spoon the sauce over the chicken evenly and Micro high for 10 minutes. (Spoon the sauce over the chicken in between also) Remove, take out the chicken pieces and keep aside.

4 Stir in the corn flour mixed with water into the gravy after taking out chicken pieces Micro high for 30 seconds. Sprinkle this gravy over the chicken and serve immediately.

CHICKEN DARBARI

Serves: 6 people
Preparation time: 19 minutes

INGREDIENTS

- *$1/_2$ kg chicken cut into curry size pieces*
- *2 green chillies crushed*
- *$1/_2$ tsp each of crushed garlic and ginger*
- *little saffron*
- *2 tbsps cream*
- *1 cup curd*
- *1 tbsp almond powder*
- *1 tbsp cashewnut powder*
- *1 tbsp raisins*
- *2 onions chopped*
- *2 potatoes cooked*
- *$1^1/_2$ tsp chilli powder*
- *$1^1/_2$ tsp salt*
- *2 tbsps ghee*
- *1 tsp garam masala*

METHOD

1 Marinate the chicken with crushed garlic, ginger, green chillies, saffron, curd, salt, chilli powder and cream 3 to 4 hours.

2 In a vessel, put ghee, Micro high 1 minute. Put chopped onion, Micro high 6 minutes.

3 Add powdered nuts, Micro high for 1 minute stirring in between.

4 Put the marinated chicken, garam masala, 1 cup hot water, Micro high for 8 minutes, stirring in between.

5 Add cooked potato pieces, raisins (if using) Micro high 3 more minutes, garnish with coriander leaves.

MANCHURIAN CHICKEN

Serves: 6 people
Preparation time: Macro + Convec-26 minutes, Dual-20 minutes,
Micro-18 minutes

INGREDIENTS

- *$1/_2$ kg boneless chicken – cut into 1 to $1^1/_2$ inch pieces*
- *1 tbsp oil*

FOR MARINATION

- *3 tbsps soya sauce*
- *2 tbsps vinegar*
- *1 tsp sherry*
- *1 tsp chilli powder or chilli sauce*
- *$1/_4$ tsp each of salt, sugar, ajinomoto*
- *garlic and ginger crushed*

METHOD

1 Wash and drain the chicken pieces and marinate in the ingredients for 3 to 4 hours.

2 Make egg batter (mix the egg and all the other ingredients for egg batter well) keep aside

3 Mix the marinated chicken pieces with egg batter.

4 Preheat the oven at 230ºC

5 Put 1 tbsp oil in a micro proof glass vessel, keep the chicken pieces in it and Micro high 6 minutes and Convec 12 minutes at 230ºC or Dual 450 for 12 minutes or Micro high 10 minutes.

6 Make Manchurian sauce (in a vessel put oil, Micro high 30 seconds, add garlic and ginger, Micro high for 1

FOR EGG BATTER

- *1 egg*
- *3 tbsps corn flour*
- *$^1/_4$ tsp each of salt and pepper*

FOR MANCHURIAN SAUCE

- *2 tbsps oil*
- *1 tbsp each of chopped garlic, ginger, green chillies and coriander leaves*
- *2 cups chicken stock*
- *1 tbsp soya sauce*
- *$^1/_4$ tsp each of salt, pepper, ajinomoto and sugar*
- *2 tbsps corn flour*

minute, add green chilies, Micro high 30 seconds. Add stock, soya sauce, salt, pepper, ajinomotto and sugar, Micro high 4 minutes) keep aside.

7 Put the chicken pieces in manchurian sauce add corn flour mixed with little water, Micro high 2 to 3 minutes stirring in between.

8 Garnish with coriander leaves.

CHICKEN CAPSICUM

Serves: 6 people
Preparation time: 15 minutes

INGREDIENTS

- *¹/₂ kg boneless chicken shredded*
- *6 tsps corn flour*
- *2 medium size capsicums*
- *2 to 3 green chillies sliced*
- *2 tbsps bamboo shoots shredded*
- *3 spring onions sliced*
- *¹/₄ tsp crushed garlic*
- *1 tsp sherry*
- *2 tsps soya sauce*
- *1 cup chicken stock*

METHOD

1 Wash the chicken and drain out water

2 Mix-in 4 tsps corn flour, salt sugar ajinomotto and pepper. Allow to stand for ¹/₂ an hour.

3 In a vessel, put 3 tbsps oil, Micro high for 1 minute, put chicken pieces, Micro high for 4 minutes or till the water dries out, stirring in between. Remove the chicken and keep aside.

4 Add 1 tbsp oil in the same vessel, add garlic, spring onion, Micro high 1 minute add beans sprout, stir, Micro high for 1 minute.

5 Add the chicken pieces, stock, soya sauce, sherry, Micro high 5 minutes.

6 Add capsicum, green chil-

- $^1/_2$ *tsp salt*
- $^1/_4$ *tsp ajinomotto*
- *Pinch of sugar and black pepper powder*
- *4 tbsps oil*

lies, Micro high 1 minute.

7 Mix the remaining corn flour with water and add to the chicken. Mix well and Micro high for 2 minutes stirring in between.

8 Serve with boiled noodles or steamed rice with chilli sauce.

CHICKEN HONGKONG

Serves: 6 people
Preparation time: 13 minutes

INGREDIENTS

- *¹/₂ kg boneless chicken*
- *3 spring onions*
- *50 gm walnuts*
- *¹/₂ tsp crushed garlic*
- *1 cup chicken stock*
- *1¹/₂ tbsp soya sauce*
- *2 tsps sherry*
- *¹/₈ tsp ajinomotto*
- *1 tsp chilli powder*
- *¹/₄ tsp each of salt and sugar*
- *4 dried red chillies*
- *2 tbsps oil*
- *2 tsps corn flour*

METHOD

1 Cut the meat into 1 inch pieces

2 Slice spring onions

3 In a bowl mix soya sauce, sherry, salt, sugar, and ajinomoto. Mix-in the chicken pieces, marinate for 2 to 4 hours.

4 In a vessel, put oil, Micro high one minute, and walnuts, Micro high one more minute and remove the walnuts.

5 Add the dried chillies, Micro high 30 seconds.

6 Add chilli powder garlic and then Micro high 30 seconds.

7 Add chicken pieces Micro high 5 minutes stirring in between.

8 Add chicken stock, Micro high 3 minutes.

9 Mix corn flour with water and add to the chicken. Mix well and Micro high 2 minutes stirring in between.

10 Garnish with spring onions and walnuts.

AMERICAN CHOPSUEY

Serves: 4 people
Preparation time: 12 minutes, 30 seconds

INGREDIENTS

- *2 tbsps oil*
- *$^1/_4$ tsp crushed garlic*
- *3 spring onions*
- *4 tbsps beans sprout*
- *4 tbsps carrots*
- *4 tbsps cabbage*
- *4 tbsps each of boneless chicken and prawns*
- *$^1/_4$ tsp salt*
- *$^1/_8$ tsp ajinomoto*
- *$^1/_2$ tsp sugar*
- *2 tsps each of soya sauce and sherry*
- *1 cup chicken stock*
- *3 tsps corn flour*
- *6 to 8 tbsps tomato ketchup*

METHOD

1 Cut the meat and vegetables into strips.

2 In a vessel, put oil, Micro high 1 minute put garlic, Micro high 30 seconds.

3 Add chicken and prawns, Micro high 3 minutes.

4 Add spring onions, Micro high 1 minute, add beans sprout, Micro high one more minute.

5 Add carrots and cabbage, chicken stock, soya sauce, sherry salt, ajinomoto, sugar and tomato ketchup. Micro high 4 minutes (if needed, Micro high one more minute to bring to a boil)

6 Mix corn flour with water add to the chopsuey, Micro high 2 minutes stirring in between.

7 Serve with crispy noodles.

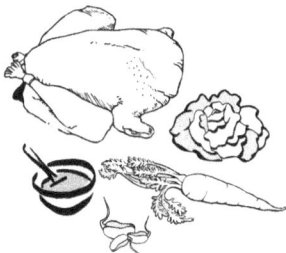

CHICKEN CHOW-MEIN

Serves: 6 people
Preparation time: 28 minutes
30 seconds

INGREDIENTS

- *1 packet noodles*
- *$\frac{1}{4}$ tsp crushed garlic*
- *2 tbsps bamboo shoots*
- *3 tbsps beans sprouts*
- *1 capsicum*
- *4 tbsps cabbage*
- *3 spring onions*
- *$\frac{1}{2}$ kg. boneless chicken*
- *1 cup chicken stock*
- *3 tsps soya sauce*
- *1 tsp sherry*
- *$\frac{1}{4}$ tsp each of salt, sugar, ajinomoto and pepper*
- *3 tsps corn flour*
- *2 tbsps oil*

METHOD

1 Take 1 litre water in a vessel and Micro high 9 minutes, when the water starts boiling, add 1 tsp oil and salt each and noodles. Micro high 4 minutes, stirring in between. Remove and strain sprinkle 1 tbsp oil on the noodles and keep aside.

2 Cut the meat and vegetables into strips.

3 In a vessel put oil, Micro high 1 minute add garlic, Micro high 30 seconds.

4 Add chicken pieces Micro high 6 minutes stirring in between.

5 Add spring onions, Micro high 1 minute, add beans sprout, Micro high 1 minute.

6 Add Bamboo shoots, capsicum, cabbage, chicken stock.

7 Mix-in sauces and seasonings, Micro high 3 to 4 minutes.

8 Mix corn flour with water, add to the chicken chow. Micro high 3 minutes stirring in between.

Serve with noodles

CHICKEN JALFRAZIE

Serves: 6 people
Preparation time: 24 minutes

INGREDIENTS

- $^1/_2$ *kg chicken*
- $^1/_2$ *tsp each of crushed garlic and ginger*
- *2 onions grated*
- *3 tomatoes blanched and chopped*
- *2 tbsps oil*
- $^3/_4$ *tsp salt and chilli powder*
- $^1/_4$ *tsp haldi powder*
- $^1/_2$ *tsp garam masala*
- *1 cup water*
- *2 eggs*

METHOD

1 In a vessel put oil Micro high 1 minute add garlic and ginger, Micro high 1 minute.

2 Add grated onion, Micro high 6 minutes, stirring in between.

3 Add chilli powder, garam masala, haldi powder salt and tomato and stir well. Micro high for 3 minutes stirring in between.

4 Add chicken, mix, Micro high 3 minutes stirring in between.

5 Add water, mix well, Micro high 3 minutes stirring in between.

6 Before serving, lightly beat 2 eggs, add it to the hot gravy and stir well. Give standing time about 10 to 15 minutes.

CHICKEN ROLL

Serves: 4 people
Preparation time: 9 minutes

INGREDIENTS

- *250 gm boneless chicken breast*
- *1 apple*
- *2 tbsps white sesame seed*
- *2 tbsps oil*
- *1 tsp corn flour*
- *1 tsp soya sauce*
- *1 tsp sherry*
- *$^1/_2$ tsp salt*
- *$^1/_8$ tsp ajinomoto*

METHOD

1 Flatten the chicken and cut thinly into 10 pieces. Mix soya sauce, sherry, salt, pepper, ajinomoto and marinate the chicken for half an hour.

2 Peel apple, cut into 2" fingers about $^1/_2$" thick.

3 Roll each chicken strip on the apple pieces. Seal the edges with corn flour roll in seasame seed.

4 Put oil in a flat dish, Micro high 1 minute.

5 Arrange the rolls in the dish, Micro high 8 minutes.

CHICKEN TIKKA

Serves: 6 people
Preparation time: Combo-18 minutes, Dual-16 minutes, Micro-10 minutes

INGREDIENTS

- *500 gm boneless chicken – cut into $1^1/_2$" pieces*
- *$^1/_2$ tsp each of crushed garlic and ginger*
- *$^1/_2$ tbsp chopped green chillies*
- *1 tbsp chopped coriander leaves*
- *$^1/_2$ tsp garam masala*
- *$^1/_2$ tsp chilli powder*
- *$^1/_2$ tsp cummin powder*
- *2 tsps coriander powder*
- *5 tsps thick curd*
- *juice of half lemon*
- *$^1/_8$ tsp orange red colour*

METHOD

1 Mix all the ingredients well except chicken and marinate the chicken with this mixture for 4 to 5 hours.

2 Preheat the oven at 230^0c and cook the marinated chicken at Combo mode at 230^0c for 18 minutes or on Dual 450 for 16 minutes turning after 8 minutes or on Micro high 10 minutes.

CHICKEN MASALA

Serves: 6 people
Preparation time: 22 minutes

INGREDIENTS

- *¹/₂ kg chicken*
- *2 onions grated*
- *3 tbsps oil*
- *75 gm cashewnut powder*
  ¹/₂ cup curd
- *3 tbsps tomato ketchup*
- *1 tsp salt*
- *¹/₂ tsp each of crushed*
  garlic and ginger
- *5 green chillies (make*
  paste)
- *1 tsp red chilli powder*
- *¹/₄ tsp turmeric powder*
- *1 tsp coriander powder*
- *¹/₂ tsp garam masala*
- *2 tbsps bread crumbs*
- *2 tbsps fresh grated*
  coconut

METHOD

1 Put oil in a vessel, Micro high 1 minute, add crushed garlic and ginger, Micro high 1 minute.

2 Add grated onion and green chilli paste, Micro high 8 minutes stirring in between.

3 Add chicken, curd, tomato ketchup, turmeric powder, chilli powder and ³/₄ cup water Micro high 8 minutes, stirring in between.

4 Add cashewnut powder bread crumbs and coconut Micro high 4 minutes, stirring in between.

5 Sprinkle garam masala and coriander leaves. Allow to stand for about 10 to 15 minutes.

AFGHANI CHICKEN

Serves: 6 people
Preparation time: 15 minutes

INGREDIENTS

- $^1/_2$ kg chicken
- $^1/_2$ cup fresh curd
- 25 gm mawa
- $^1/_2$ tsp each of crushed garlic and ginger
- 4 green chillies sliced
- 2 tbsps ghee
- 2 onions birishta (onion fried to dark brown colour)
- 1 tsp chilli sauce
- 25 gm cashewnuts
- $^1/_2$ tsp haldi powder
- 3 cloves
- 4 cardamoms
- 1" piece cinnamon
- 2 tomatoes
- $^3/_4$ tsp salt
- 2 tsp grated cheese

METHOD

1 In a vessel put the ghee Micro high 1 minute, put chicken and Micro high 4 minutes stirring in between.

2 Add garlic, ginger, green chilli haldi powder, salt and ground tomatoes (grind tomato and garam masala together) Micro high 3 minutes.

3 Grate mawa, mix with curd and add to the chicken along with onion birishta Micro high 6 minutes.

4 Add chilli sauce and grated cheese Micro high 1 minute.

5 Give standing time about 10 minutes.

GREEN CHICKEN

Serves: 6 people
Preparation time: 15 minutes

INGREDIENTS

- *½ kg chicken — cut to pieces*
- *1 cup curd*
- *½ tsp each of garlic and ginger paste*
- *1 tsp green chilli paste*
- *¾ tsp salt*
- *2 tbsps cashewnuts*
- *1 bunch (2 cups) coriander leaves*
- *2 tbsps oil*

METHOD

1 Grind cashewnuts and coriander leaves together and keep aside.

2 In a vessel, put oil, Micro high 1 minute

3 Add ginger garlic, Micro high 1 minute

4 Put chicken, green chilli paste, stir and Micro high 4 minutes, stirring in between.

5 Add salt, curd cook on Micro high 4 minutes

6 Add coriander/cashewnuts paste (if required little water can be added) Micro high 5 minutes, give standing time for about 10 minutes.

CHICKEN HYDERABADI

Serves: 6 people
Preparation time: 19 minutes

INGREDIENTS

- *¹/₂ kg chicken*
- *50 gm coconut grated*
- *1 tsp poppy seed (khuskhus)*
- *1 tbsp groundnuts*
- *4 to 5 flakes garlic*
- *1" piece ginger*
- *3 tsps coriander powder*
- *1 tsp chilli powder*
- *1 tsp salt*
- *pinch of turmeric powder*
- *3 cloves*
- *2 pieces cinnamon*
- *2 cardamoms*
- *2 onions*
- *2 tbsp oil*
- *coriander leaves to garnish*

METHOD

1 Cut the chicken into small pieces and smear it with chilli powder, turmeric and salt.

2 Grind together all the remaining ingredients except onion and coriander leaves, to a paste.

3 In a vessel, put oil, Micro high 1 minute. Put chopped onion Micro high 5 minutes.

4 Add the ground paste Micro high 3 minutes stirring in between.

5 Add chicken pieces, 1 cup water, Micro high 10 minutes garnish with coriander leaves.

CHICKEN KASHMIRI DUM

Serves: 10 people
Preparation time: 29 minutes 30 seconds

INGREDIENTS

- *1 kg chicken*
- *3 tbsps oil*
- *2 blanched tomatoes*
- *2 big onions grated*
- *10 cashewnuts – powdered*
- *10 flakes garlic – crushed to a paste*
- *1" piece ginger crushed to a paste*
- *1½ tsp salt*

- *1 tsp jeera*
- *⅛ tsp mustard seed*
- *¼ tsp pepper*
- *3 pieces cinnamon*
- *4 cloves*
- *12 kashmiri chillies*

combine and grind to a paste

METHOD

1 Cut the chicken into small pieces and smear it with salt, little turmeric powder and keep aside.

2 Put oil in a vessel and Micro high 1½ minute. Put onions Micro high 8 minutes, stirring in between.

3 Add garlic ginger paste Micro high 2 minutes.

4 Add ground masala, Micro high 3 minutes stirring in between.

5 Add tomato, cashewnut powder, Micro high 3 minutes. Put the chicken pieces in 2 cups hot water Micro high 12 minutes stirring in between give standing time of 10 to 15 minutes.

CHICKEN DO PIAZZA

Serves: 6 people
Preparation time: 23 minutes

INGREDIENTS

- *¹/₂ kg chicken*
- *2 large onions*
- *5 green chillies*
- *1 tsp chilli powder*
- *1 tsp coriander powder*
- *¹/₂ tsp turmeric powder*
- *¹/₂ pepper powder*
- *³/₄ tsp salt*
- *2 tbsps ghee*
- *1" piece ginger*
- *4 cloves garlic*
- *garam masala*
- *4 cloves*
- *2 cardamoms*
- *¹/₂ tsp sounf*

METHOD

1 Heat 1 tbsp ghee on Micro high for 1 minutes, add garam masala, Micro high 1 minute.

2 Cut garlic ginger and green chillies lengthwise and add to garam masala Micro high 1 minute.

3 Add 1 onion sliced –Micro high 3 minutes, mix chilli, coriander, turmeric powder with little water and add to the above mixture. Micro high 2 minutes.

4 Add chicken pieces salt, pepper, one cup hot water, Micro high 10 minutes. Garnish with coriander leaves.

5 Put the remaining ghee in a vessel, fry the remaining one onion on Micro high for 6 minutes and garnish the chicken it.

RED MASALA CHICKEN

Serves: 6 people
Preparation time: 21 minutes

INGREDIENTS

- $^1/_2$ kg chicken – cut into curry size pieces
- 4 to 5 kashmiri chillies
- 1 tsp chilli powder
- 1" piece ginger
- 4 cloves garlic
- 1 tsp cummin seed
- 2 small cardamoms
- 2" piece cinnamon
- 3 cloves
- $^1/_4$ tsp pepper corn
- 4 cashewnuts
- $^1/_4$ kg tomato puree
- $^1/_2$ tsp sugar
- 3 onions
- 1 tsp salt
- $^1/_2$ lime
- 2 tbsps oil

METHOD

1 Cut onion finely.

2 Grind the spices, green masala and cashewnuts finely (kashmiri chilli, chilli powder, cummin seed cardamom cinnamon, cloves, pepper, ginger and garlic).

3 In a vessel, put 2 tbsp oil Micro high 1 minute, add onion Micro high 6 minutes.

4 Add the ground masala, Micro high 4 minutes stirring in between.

5 Add chicken pieces, tomato puree, salt, sugar and $^1/_2$ cup warm water, cook on Micro high 10 minutes covering partly.

6 Add lime juice, mix nicely and give 10 minutes standing time.

GOAN CHICKEN CURRY

Serves: 6 people
Preparation time: 14 minutes

INGREDIENTS

- *¹/₂ kg chicken cut into curry size pieces*
- *1 coconut — grated*
- *1 tbsp coriander seeds*
- *¹/₂ tsp cummin seeds*
- *6 red chillies*
- *5 cloves*
- *3 pieces cinnamon*
- *¹/₄ tsp methi (fenugreek) seeds*
- *1 tbsp tamarind pulp*
- *2 tbsps ghee*
- *¹/₄ tsp turmeric powder*
- *1 tsp salt*

METHOD

1 Grind the following ingredients to a smooth paste, ¹/₂ coconut grated, coriander seed, mustard seeds, red chillies cloves, cinnamon and fenugreek seeds.

2 Squeeze out the milk from the remaining grated coconut (milk 1-keepside) after squeezing out the milk, add one cup water to the coconut, grind and squeeze out the milk (milk 2).

3 Add tamarind pulp to milk 1 and keep aside.

4 In a vessel, Micro high ghee for 1 minute put the ground paste, Micro high 3 minutes stirring in between.

5 Add turmeric, chicken pieces, salt and milk 2 cover partly, Micro high 10 minutes.

6 Take out from the oven and mix milk 1 cover and keep for 10 minutes.

FISH
PREPARATION

The combination of your favourite fish with various garnishing makes wonderful and tasty dishes that are unbelievably easy to do. You can make these recipes when you want to cook a very special dish for your family or when you want to impress your guests.

CHUTNEY STUFFED TANDOORI POMFRET

Serves: 4 people
Preparation time: Combo-12 minutes, Dual-12 minutes, Micro-8 minutes

INGREDIENTS

- *1 medium size pomfret*
- *¹/₂ the quantity of tandoori curd masala (refer ingredients for tandoori chicken)*
- *green chutney*

METHOD

1 Make the green chutney by grinding together one bunch coriander leaves, few green chillies, one small piece ginger, 4 to 5 flakes garlic, ¹/₄ tsp sugar, ¹/₈ tsp jeera, few mint leaves (optional) and salt for taste.

2 Remove the centre bone of the fish, make fine cuts on the flesh, stuff with chutney.

3 Apply tandoori curd masala on top and marinate for 1 to 2 hours.

4 Preheat the oven at 200°C and cook on Combo mode at 200°C for 12 minutes or on, Dual mode 150 for 12 minutes turning after 5 minutes or on Micro high 8 minutes.

MASALA POMFRET

Serves: 4 people
Preparation time: Combo-12 minutes, Dual-12 minutes, Micro-8 minutes

INGREDIENTS

- *1 medium size pomfret*
- *3 or 4 cloves garlic*
- *¹/₂ inch piece ginger*
- *1 onion chopped*
- *2 tsps roasted coriander powder*
- *¹/₄ tsp turmeric powder*
- *¹/₂ tsp salt*
- *1 tsp chilli powder*
- *1 tsp roasted cummin seed powder*

combine and grind to a paste

FOR STUFFING

- *2 green chillies chopped*
- *1 onion chopped*
- *2 tbsps finely chopped coriander leaves*

METHOD

1 Clean and dry the fish make gashes on both sides.

2 Take half of the ground paste, combine with stuffing mixture and fill inside the fish.

3 Rub the remaining paste on both the sides of the fish.

4 Leave to marinate for 2 hours.

5 In a dish put 1 tbsp oil, keep the fish inside, sprinkle 1 tbsp oil on top.

6 Preheat the oven at 200°C and cook on combo mode at 200°C for 12 minutes or on Dual mode 150 for 12 minutes turning after 6 minutes or on Micro high 8 minutes.

FISH WITH SAUCE

Serves: 4 people
Preparation time: 15 minutes

INGREDIENTS

- *1 large size pomfret*
- *2 onions*
- *4 to 5 cloves garlic*
- *6 green chillies*
- *1 inch piece ginger*
- *1 tsp sugar*
- *$\frac{1}{2}$ tsp cummin seeds*
- *2 tbsps vinegar*
- *2 eggs*
- *3 tbsps salt*
- *1 tsp pepper*
- *coriander leaves –*
  chopped

METHOD

1 Slice the fish into pieces.

2 Chop onions very finely.

3 Grind garlic, chillies, ginger and cummin seeds to a smooth paste.

4 Keep oil in a vessel and Micro high 1 minute. Add onions and Micro high 2 minutes.

5 Add the paste (see step 3) Micro high 3 minutes stirring in between.

6 Add 1 cup water or stock and mix well.

7 Cook on Micro high for 4 minutes or till it boils.

8 Blend maida with little water to a smooth paste and mix Micro high 2 minutes stirring in between.

9 Put the fish inside, add salt and pepper and Micro high 3 to 4 minutes or till the fish is cooked.

10 Beat eggs, vinegar and sugar together.

11 Remove the dish from oven, pour in the egg mixture stir gently.

12 Mix in the chopped coriander leaves.

PRAWNS IN SCHEZWAN GARLIC SAUCE

Serves: 4 people
Preparation time:
11 minutes 30 seconds

INGREDIENTS

- *2 tbsp oil*
- *1 tbsp chopped garlic*
- *1 tsp chilli powder*
- *$\frac{1}{2}$ cup tomato ketchup*
- *$\frac{1}{2}$ cup tomato puree*
- *1 tsp each of soya sauce and sherry*
- *$\frac{1}{4}$ tsp each of salt and ajinomoto*
- *2 tsps corn flour*
- *1 cup chicken stock or water*
- *250 gm prawns*

METHOD

1 Make egg batter (1 egg, 3 tbsp corn flour, $\frac{1}{4}$ tsp each of salt and pepper).

2 Mix-in prawns and marinate for 15 to 20 minutes.

3 In a vessel, put oil, add the marinated prawns Micro high 4 to 5 minutes stirring in between.

4 Remove the prawns and keep aside.

5 Add 1 tbsp oil to the vessel, Micro high 1 minute, add chilli powder and garlic, Micro high 30 seconds.

6 Add tomato ketchup, tomato puree and chicken stock or water, Micro high 4 to 5 minutes.

7 Add soya sauce, sherry, salt and ajinomoto.

8 Mix corn flour with water and add to the sauce along with prawns, Micro high 2 minutes. Garnish with spring onions.

MANDARIAN FISH

Serves: 4 people
Preparation time: Combo-17 minutes 30 seconds, Dual-17 minutes
30 seconds, Micro-15 minutes 30 seconds

INGREDIENTS

- *1 medium size pomfret*
- *$\frac{1}{4}$ tsp each of salt and pepper*
- *$\frac{1}{8}$ tsp ajinomoto*
- *1 egg*
- *3 tbsps flour (maida)*

SAUCE

- *6 tbsps vinegar*
- *2 tbsps sugar*
- *2 tsps each of soya sauce and tomato sauce*

METHOD

1 Make deep cuts on both sides of the fish wash and drain out water.

2 Make egg batter by mixing egg, flour, salt pepper and ajinomoto.

3 Coat the fish with egg batter and leave for 15 to 20 minutes.

4 In a flat oven proof glass dish, put 1 tbsp oil keep the fish in it.

5 Preheat the oven at 230°C and cook the fish on Combo mode at 230°C for 10 minutes or on Dual mode 450 for 10 minutes turning after 5 minutes or Micro high 8 minutes.

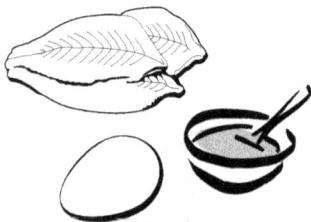

- *$\frac{1}{4}$ tsp each of salt and pepper*
- *$\frac{1}{8}$ tsp ajinomoto*
- *1 tsp chilli powder*
- *$\frac{3}{4}$ cup chicken stock*
- *3 tsps corn flour*
- *1 tbsp oil*

METHOD FOR SAUCE

In a vessel put oil, Micro high 30 seconds add chilli powder, mix well add the chicken stock and then all the other ingredients for the sauce except corn flour. Micro high 3 minutes, stirring in between. Mix corn flour with water and add to the sauce. Micro high another 2 minutes stirring in between.

Place the fish in a flat serving dish and pour the sauce over it.

SWEET AND SOUR PRAWN

Serves: 6 people
Preparation time: 12 minutes

INGREDIENTS

- *1 cup chicken stock or water*
- *6 tbsps vinegar*
- *3 tbsps sugar*
- *2 tbsps tomato ketchup*
- *1 tbsp soya sauce*
- *2 tbsps oil*
- *2 tbsps corn flour*
- *$\frac{1}{2}$ tsp each of salt and ajinomoto*
- *1 tsp chilli powder*
- *250 gm prawns*

METHOD

1 Make egg batter by mixing one egg, 3 tbsps corn flour, $\frac{1}{4}$ tsp each of salt and pepper.

2 Add the prawns to the egg batter and allow to stand for 15 to 20 minutes.

3 In a vessel put 2 tbsp oil, Micro high 1 minute, add prawns, Micro high 4 to 5 minutes stirring in between. Remove the prawns from the vessel and keep aside.

METHOD FOR SAUCE

Cur spring onions, tomato, capsicum and pineapple into big pieces. In a vessel, put oil, Micro high 1 minute, add spring onions, Micro high 1 minute. Take out the vessel add chilli powder mix well, add chicken stock or water,

VEGETABLES FOR SAUCE

- *2 spring onions*
- *1 capsicum*
- *1 tomato*
- *2 rings of pineapple*

vinegar, sugar, tomato sauce, soya sauce, stir Micro high 3 minutes stirring in between. Add salt, ajinomoto, stir well. Mix corn flour with water and add along with vegetable and prawns, mix well Micro high 2 minutes stirring in between.

DAHI FISH

Serves: 6 people
Preparation time: 8 minutes 30 seconds

INGREDIENTS

- $^1/_2$ kg fish pieces
- $^1/_2$ cup fresh curd
- 2 tbsps oil
- 1 big onion
- 1" piece ginger
- 8 green chillies
- 3 pieces cinnamon
- 3 cloves
- 2 cardamoms
- $^1/_4$ tsp pepper corn
- pinch of sugar
- 1 tsp salt
- 2 black cardamoms

METHOD

1 Grind green chillies, onion and ginger to a fine paste. Add curd, sugar, salt to the ground paste.

2 Apply this paste to the fish pieces. Pour 1 tbsp oil on top.

3 Micro high the remaining oil in vessel for 30 seconds. Add whole garam masala then pour this on the fish evenly. Cook on Micro high for 3 minutes, stir in between gently. Then Micro low (keep at half of the maximum power shown in the oven) for 5 minutes covering partly.

CURRIED BOMBAY DUCK

Serves: 6 people
Preparation time: 14 minutes

INGREDIENTS

- *6 bombay ducks (bombil)*
- *1" piece ginger*
- *5 to 6 kashmiri chillies*
- *1 tsp pepper corn*
- *1/4 tsp turmeric powder*
- *4 to 5 cloves garlic*
- *225 gms tomatoes*
- *1 small lime size tamarind*
- *1 onion sliced*
- *1 tsp salt*
- *2 tbsps oil*
- *few coriander leaves*

METHOD

1 Blanch the tomatoes and make a pulp.

2 Soak the tamarind in little water and grind it along with chillies, garlic, pepper corn, turmeric and ginger.

3 In a vessel, Micro high oil for a minute add sliced onion, Micro high 4 minutes. Add the ground masala and Micro high for 4 minutes stirring in between.

4 Add tomato pulp and salt, Micro high 3 minutes stirring in between.

5 Add fish and Micro high 2 to 3 minutes. Give standing time 5 to 10 minutes.

PRAWN CURRY WITH COCONUT MILK

Serves: 6 people
Preparation time: 16 minutes

INGREDIENTS

- $^1/_2$ kg shelled prawns
- 1 coconut grated
- 2 onions cut fine
- 1 tsp salt

GRIND TO A PASTE

- 8 red chillies
- $^1/_2$" piece turmeric
- 1 tsp cummin seed
- 5 cloves garlic

METHOD

1 Grind the coconut with 1 cup of water squeeze out thick milk and keep aside. Add $1^1/_2$ cup water to the coconut and squeeze out thinner milk.

2 Mix the masala paste with the thinner milk.

3 In a vessel put 2 tbsp oil Micro high 1 minute, put onions, Micro high 5 minutes.

4 Add the coconut milk with masala paste, prawns and Micro high 8 minutes.

5 Add the thick coconut milk, Micro high for 2 minutes. Serve with rice.

FISH CURRY

Serves: 6 people
Preparation time: 12 minutes

INGREDIENTS

- $^1/_2$ kg pomfret
- $^3/_4$ tsp salt
- $^1/_2$ coconut grated
- 8 red chillies
- $^1/_2$ tsp jeera
- $^1/_2$ tsp turmeric powder
- lime size tamarind

Grind to a paste

- 3 to 4 green chillies
- 1 onion chopped
- $^1/_2$ piece ginger

Crush together

METHOD

1 Mix the masala paste and the crushed masala together in a vessel with 1 cup water and cook on Micro high for about 6 minutes, add salt.

2 Clean and cut fish and cook on Micro high for about 4 minutes. Followed by Micro low (Half the maximum power reading) for 2 minutes.

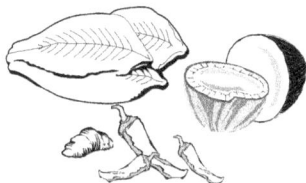

KERALA FISH CURRY

Serves: 6 people
Preparation time: 10 minutes

INGREDIENTS

- *500 gm pomfret pieces*
- *20 gm kokam or Kodampuli or tamarind*
- *4 tbsps coconut oil*
- *3 to 4 green chillies slit*
- *1 tsp salt*
- *few curry leaves*

FOR MASALA

- *$\frac{1}{2}$ coconut*
- *10 red chillies*
- *$\frac{1}{2}$ tsp turmeric*
- *$\frac{1}{2}$ tsp cummin seeds*
- *4 to 5 flakes garlic*
- *$\frac{1}{2}$" piece ginger*
- *1 small onion*

Grind together

METHOD

1 Soak kokam in little warm water.

2 heat oil on Micro high for 1 minute. Add curry leaves and ground masala Micro-high 3 minutes stirring in between.

3 Add fish, green chillies, kokam water, salt, and enough water to cover the fish.

4 Cook on Micro high 4 minutes followed by Micro low (half the maximum power reading) 2 minutes.

EGG
PREPARATION

Egg lovers from all over will love these very elegant and tasteful dish. Very different and distinguished in taste you can prepare them with gravy or dry. Fast to cook and healthy to eat these quick egg recipes will make a good breakfast, lunch or dinner.

SCRAMBLED EGG WITH SHRIMPS

Serves: 3 people
Preparation time: 9 minutes

INGREDIENTS

- *100 gm shelled shrimp*
- *2 tbsps butter*
- *4 eggs*
- *4 tbsps milk*
- *3 to 4 green chillies finely chopped*
- *few coriander leaves chopped*
- *$\frac{1}{2}$ tsp salt*
- *$\frac{1}{2}$ tsp pepper*

METHOD

1 In a vessel, put butter Micro high for 1 minute.

2 Put shrimps, cook on Micro high 3 minutes.

3 Beat the eggs with milk, salt, pepper and green chilli and add to the shrimp.

4 Micro high for 2 minutes stirring after one minute.

5 Cook on Micro low power (half of the maximum power reading) for 3 minutes.

6 This can be served on a toast.

EGG CURRY WITH PEAS

Serves: 6 people
Preparation time: 28 minutes

INGREDIENTS

- *6 eggs — hard boiled*
- *2 tbsps ghee*
- *2 big onions chopped*
- *2" piece cinnamon*
- *2 bay leaves*
- *2 tbsp coriander powder*
- *$^1/_4$ tsp turmeric powder*
- *1 tsp garam masala powder*
- *$^1/_2$ tsp crushed ginger and garlic each*
- *3 tomatoes – blanched and chopped*
- *$^3/_4$ tsp salt*
- *$^1/_2$ tsp chilli powder*
- *1 cup green peas*

METHOD

1 Take six eggs in a vessel and pour sufficient water to immerse all the eggs completely. (Eggs and water should be at room temperature) Micro high 8 minutes, cool and remove the shell.

2 Cut in halves lengthwise

3 In a vessel put ghee Micro high 1 minute add onions garlic and ginger Micro high 6 minutes, stirring in between.

4 Add cinnamon, bay leaves and powdered spices Micro high 1 minute stirring in between.

5 Put the chopped tomatoes Micro high 2 minutes, stirring after one minute.

6 Add 1 cup water peas partly cover and Micro high 5 minutes.

7 Put the egg Micro low (half of the maximum power reading shown in the oven) for 5 minutes.

EGG CURRY WITH COCONUT MILK

Serves: 6 people
Preparation time: 19 minutes

INGREDIENTS

- *6 eggs – hard boiled*
- *1 tsp cummin seeds*
- *5 red chillies*
- *1 big onion*
- *3 cloves garlic*
- *1 tsp mustard seeds*
- *$\frac{1}{2}$ cup coconut milk (grate half coconut of good size add $\frac{1}{4}$ cup water grind and squeeze out milk)*
- *$\frac{1}{2}$ tsp salt*

METHOD

1 Grind onion garlic mustard seeds cummin seeds, chilli and salt.

2 In a vessel put 1 tbsp ghee, Micro high 1 minute put the paste Micro high 4 minutes stirring in between.

3 Remove the shell and add the eggs halved, cook on Micro low (half of the maximum power reading shown in the oven) 4 minutes, stirring in between.

4 Add coconut milk Micro low ($\frac{1}{3}$ of the maximum power reading) 2 minutes.

EGG VINDALOO

Serves: 6 people
Preparation time: 15 minutes

INGREDIENTS

- *6 eggs – hard boiled and shelled*
- *2 onions*
- *4 cloves garlic*
- *1" piece ginger*
- *4 red chillies*
- *1 tsp cummin seeds*
- *1" piece cinnamon*
- *4 to 5 tbsp vinegar*
- *1 tsp sugar*
- *½ tsp garam masala*
- *1 tsp salt*
- *½ cup water*
- *2 tbsp ghee*

METHOD

1 Grind red chillies, garlic, ginger, cummin seed and cinnamon with little vinegar.

2 Mix sugar add the remaining vinegar.

3 In a vessel, put ghee, Micro high one minute, put onion, Micro high 5 minutes stirring in between.

4 Add the ground paste, salt, Micro high 3 minutes, stirring in between.

5 Add vinegar/sugar mixture garam masala and water. Micro high 2 minutes.

6 Add the eggs Micro low (half of he maximum power reading) 4 minutes.

CAKES

Nothing can be more entrancing, more indulgent and more satisfying than a slice of cake. Complete that special meal or a celebration with these delicious easy-to-make cake recipies.

QUICK CHOCOLATE CAKE

Serves: 8 people
Preparation time: Micro+Convec-15 minutes, Dual-8 minutes,
Micro-8 minutes

INGREDIENTS

- *1 cup maida (flour)*
- *³/₄ cup curd*
- *2 eggs*
- *¹/₄ cup refined oil*
- *¹/₄ cup coco powder*
- *³/₄ tsp soda-bi-carb*
- *pinch of salt*
- *¹/₂ tsp vanilla essence*
- *³/₄ cup powdered sugar*

METHOD

1 In a bowl, mix all ingredients together beat with hand beater till well blended. If electric beater is used beat at low speed for 1 minute then 3 minutes and 3 minutes at high speed. Do not over beat the mixture. Pour the mixture into a greased vessel.

2 Preheat the oven at 230ºC, Micro high 3 minutes and Convec 230ºC for 12 minutes or on Dual mode 450ºC for 8 minutes or Micro high 8 minutes.

HEALTH CAKE

Serves: 16 people
Preparation time: Micro+Convec-18 minutes, Dual-9 minutes,
Micro-9 minutes

INGREDIENTS

- *1¹/₄ cup wheat flour*
- *1 tsp baking powder*
- *¹/₄ tsp soda-bi-carb*
- *pinch of salt*
- *1 cup sugar powder*
- *3 eggs*
- *1¹/₄ cup refined oil*
- *1¹/₄ cup finely grated carrot*
- *1 tsp vanilla essence*
- *¹/₄ tsp nutmeg powder*
- *100 gm tutifruiti + raisins + cashewnuts mixture*

METHOD

1 Sieve together wheat flour, baking powder soda-bi-carb, nutmeg powder and salt thrice, mix-in dry fruits and keep aside.

2 Cream the powdered sugar, oil and egg yolk in a vessel, add grated carrot and vanilla essence, mix well. Pour in the wheat flour mixture. Lastly pour stiffly beaten egg white.

3 Transfer to a greased dish. Preheat the oven at 230°C, bake the cake on Micro high 4 minutes and Convec 14 to 15 minutes at 230°C or Dual mode 450°C for 9 to 10 minutes or Micro high for 9 to 10 minutes.

ORANGE COCONUT CAKE

Serves: 16 people
Preparation time: Micro+Convec-15 minutes, Dual-8 minutes,
Micro-8 minutes

INGREDIENTS

- *¹/₂ cup dessicated coconut*
- *¹/₂ cup milk*
- *125 gm butter*
- *1 cup powdered sugar*
- *1 tbsp grated orange rind*
- *2 eggs*
- *1 cup maida*
- *few drops orange essence and orange colour*
- *1¹/₂ tsp baking powder*

METHOD

1 Combine coconut and milk in a bowl allow to stand for 1 hour.

2 Sieve maida with baking powder

3 Cream the butter and sugar until light and flufly.

4 Add orange rind.

5 Beat-in-eggs one at a time. Add essence and colour.

6 Stir in seived flour coconut/milk mixture in small quantities alternatively.

7 Pour in to a greased vessel, preheat the oven at 230°C bake the cake at Micro high 3 minutes and Convec at 230°C for 12 minute or on Dual mode 450°C for 8 minutes or on Micro high 8 minutes

MAWA CAKE

Serves: 8 people
Preparation time: Micro+Convec-12 minutes, Dual-7 minutes,
Micro-7 minutes

INGREDIENTS

- *50 gm flour (maida)*
- *$1/4$ tsp baking powder*
- *$1/8$ tsp cardamom powder*
- *$1/8$ tsp nutmeg powder*
- *50 gm mawa grated*
- *50 gm margarin*
- *$1/4$ cup milk at room temperature*
- *50 gm sugar powder*
- *2 eggs*
- *$1/4$ tsp vanilla essence*

METHOD

1 Sieve flour baking powder cardamom powder and nutmeg powder, together and mix-in mawa.

2 Cream the margarin, add milk and beat.

3 Add sugar gradually and continue creaming until light and fluffy.

4 Beat the eggs well and add gradually add essence.

5 Pour in flour and mawa mixture, transfer to a greased vessel. Preheat the oven at 230°C, Micro high 2 minutes and Convec at 230°C for 10 minutes or on Dual mode 450 for 7 minutes or Micro high 7 minutes.

PICKLE

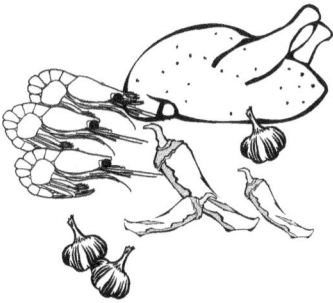

Whether they are sweet, sour, spicy or a combination of any of these tastes, they sure do make our mouths water, time and time again. Here are two tasty and tongue tickling pickle recipes to complete your meal with a tang.

PRAWNS PICKLE

Quantity: 1 small bottle
Preparation time: 13 minutes

INGREDIENTS

- *¹/₂ kg prawns*
- *30 gm chilli powder*
- *15 gm green chillies*
- *10 gm ginger*
- *30 gm garlic*
- *30 to 40 gm salt*
- *120 ml seasame oil (til oil)*
- *200 ml white Vinegar*
- *1 tsp mustard seed*
- *few curry leaves*
- *6 to 8 red chillies*
- *¹/₂ tsp pepper corns*
- *¹/₂ tsp turmeric*
- *2 tsp salt*

Grind to a paste

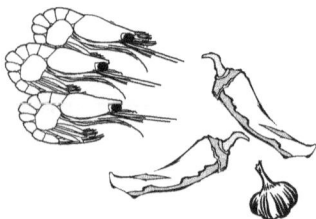

METHOD

1 Shell the prawns, remove veins, wash and drain using cloth.

2 Smear the ground paste on prawns.

3 Put 50 ml oil in a vessel, Micro high 2 minutes.

4 Add prawns cook on Micro high 4 minutes. Partly covering and stirring in between.

5 Peel and slice garlic and ginger and slit green chillies.

6 In a vessel, heat the remaining oil on Micro high 2 minutes. Micro high one minute, and add curry leaves, green chillies, garlic, ginger. Micro high 2 minutes, stirring in between.

7 Remove the vessel from the oven, add chilli powder, stir well, add vinegar and salt, Micro high 2 minutes, cool and add prawns.

HOT CHICKEN PICKLE

Quantity: 1 small bottle
Preparation time: 20 minutes

INGREDIENTS

- *500 gm boneless chicken*
- *100 gm white vinegar*
- *20 gm red chillies*
- *2 tsps mustard seeds*
- *1 tsp fenugreek seeds*
- *50 gm tamarind pulp*
- *125 ml seasame oil*
- *1 to 1$^1/_2$ tbsp salt*
- *6 to 8 flakes garlic*
- *pinch of sodium benzoate*
- *$^1/_2$ tsp asafoetida (hing) powder*

METHOD

1 In a vessel, put chillies, fenugreek, mustard and asafoetida, Micro high 1 minute and grind to a powder.

2 Slice the garlic cut the chicken into small pieces, wash and drain.

3 Heat oil on Micro high 2 minutes, put garlic, Micro high 2 minutes, add the chicken, Micro high 8 minutes, add salt tamarind and garlic Micro high 2 minutes.

4 Add vinegar and keep on Microlow (Half of the maximum power reading) for 5 minutes.

5 Remove, cool, sprinkle sodium benzoate on top.

JAICO PUBLISHING HOUSE

Elevate Your Life. Transform Your World.

ESTABLISHED IN 1946, Jaico Publishing House is home to world-transforming authors such as Sri Sri Paramahansa Yogananda, Osho, The Dalai Lama, Sri Sri Ravi Shankar, Robin Sharma, Deepak Chopra, Jack Canfield, Eknath Easwaran, Devdutt Pattanaik, Khushwant Singh, John Maxwell, Brian Tracy and Stephen Hawking.

Our late founder Mr. Jaman Shah first established Jaico as a book distribution company. Sensing that independence was around the corner, he aptly named his company Jaico ('Jai' means victory in Hindi). In order to service the significant demand for affordable books in a developing nation, Mr. Shah initiated Jaico's own publications. Jaico was India's first publisher of paperback books in the English language.

While self-help, religion and philosophy, mind/body/spirit, and business titles form the cornerstone of our non-fiction list, we publish an exciting range of travel, current affairs, biography, and popular science books as well. Our renewed focus on popular fiction is evident in our new titles by a host of fresh young talent from India and abroad. Jaico's recently established Translations Division translates selected English content into nine regional languages.

Jaico's Higher Education Division (HED) is recognized for its student-friendly textbooks in Business Management and Engineering which are in use countrywide.

In addition to being a publisher and distributor of its own titles, Jaico is a major national distributor of books of leading international and Indian publishers. With its headquarters in Mumbai, Jaico has branches and sales offices in Ahmedabad, Bangalore, Bhopal, Bhubaneswar, Chennai, Delhi, Hyderabad, Kolkata and Lucknow.

SINCE 1946

www.ingramcontent.com/pod-product-compliance
Lightning Source LLC
La Vergne TN
LVHW011210080426
835508LV00007B/716